Richard Saul Ferguson, Alexander Ansted

**Carlisle Cathedral**

Richard Saul Ferguson, Alexander Ansted

**Carlisle Cathedral**

ISBN/EAN: 9783744716857

Printed in Europe, USA, Canada, Australia, Japan

Cover: Foto ©Andreas Hilbeck / pixelio.de

More available books at **www.hansebooks.com**

Carlisle Cathedral
North-West view

# Carlisle Cathedral

*By*

The Worshipful
R. S. Ferguson, F.S.A.

*Chancellor of Carlisle*

Illustrated by
Alexander Ansted

London : Isbister & Co. Ltd.
15 & 16 Tavistock Street Covent Garden
MDCCCXCVIII

# Carlisle Cathedral

I F it were possible, by the wave of a
magician's wand, to sweep away the
mighty mass of made earth and buildings, past and present, that cover the original
surface of the site on which the city of
Carlisle now stands, a spectator stationed
beyond the web of railway lines that lie to
westward of the Cathedral—standing, for in-
stance, where the great smoke-stalk known
as Dixon's chimney rears its head—would
see a long hill of New Red sandstone rising
gently from the south end of the present
city of Carlisle (from far to the south of the
present central railway station), to a head on

which now stands the Cathedral of Carlisle. Northwards of this, beyond a deep ravine, he would see a second hill rising still northwards to a second and higher head, and looking out towards the north like a lion— the Castle Hill of Carlisle, a natural fortress to guard the waths or fords through the beautiful river running under it from east to west through a broad expanse of marsh and willow-bed.

In the foreground of his view he would see the precipitous cliffs into which these two hills break on their eastern sides, as they tower above a second and lesser river, which contributes its waters to the first a little to the west and north of the Castle Hill. Could our imaginary spectator, by some magician's flying carpet, raise himself to the level of the top of the great chimney-stalk, he would see a third and yet smaller river flowing into the first, some way to the eastward of the Castle Hill. He would notice that to the south these two lesser rivers so nearly coalesce as to enclose the Castle and Cathedral hills in a quasi-island. He would notice patches of heather growing on these two hills and in the ravine between them, while frequent springs burst out, even on their highest points. He would, perhaps, see a few wretched wigwams on the Castle Hill, whose scantily-clad inhabitants were, some fishing for salmon in the rivers, others, armed with arrows tipped or pointed with bone, hunting in the ravine and on the Cathedral Hill for small animals and birds.

Now the above is not the vain imagining of a dreaming antiquary. The three rivers —the Eden, the Caldew, and the Petteril— still enclose the Castle and Cathedral hills in a quasi-island. The precipitous cliffs of these hills are still to be seen in Devonshire Walk under the Castle, and in the West Walls under the Cathedral. The ravine is filled up with *débris* and building rubbish, and the stuff that ever accumulates in ancient cities ; but in digging the foundations for the

entrance to Tullie House, midway between
the Cathedral and the Castle, seventeen feet
of made earth had to be worked through
before the original surface of the undisturbed
soil was reached. That surface was covered
with dried heather, a sod of which is preserved in the museum in Tullie House.
The presence of the hunter was proved by
finding on the heathery surface the bone-tip
of one of his arrows. The present water-
logged condition of the soil at no great
depth proves the existence of the many
springs which even yet survive to trouble
building contractors.

It is foreign to our purpose to go into the
history of these two hills—the Castle Hill and
the Cathedral Hill of Carlisle ; we must just
state what is necessary for the understanding
of the story of the hill on which the Cathedral
of Carlisle stands. Briefly, then, we suggest,
for we cannot say for certain, that the great
Roman general Agricola built a fort of stone
at Stanwix on the north side of the River

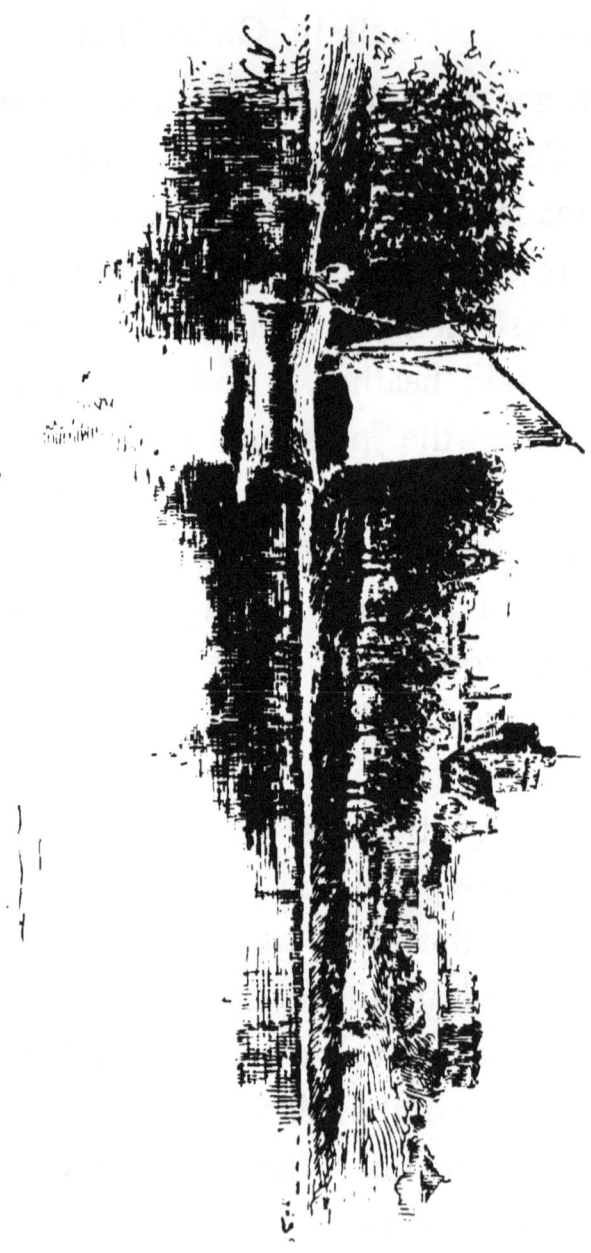

View from Stanwix

Eden—on another hill, where the church of Stanwix, conspicuous by its tower, now stands. Suburbs soon gathered on the cramped slope between the fort and the river. As the settlers increased, more room was required, and they built upon the Cathedral Hill of Carlisle, and protected themselves with a stout palisade of oak, whose remains, deep underground, have at various times been disinterred. Bad times came, and in the troubles that preceded the arrival of the Emperor Hadrian in A.D. 120, Luguvallium—for so the Romans named the town on the Cathedral Hill—was burnt ; it lay desolate and waste when that Emperor visited the site. With the return of peace and security, Luguvallium grew up upon a large scale and became a city of luxury, covering a considerable area, and having an extensive cemetery to its south, situate right and left of the highway, and extending from the present Assize Courts almost to the River Petteril. Of the Roman and British life of this city we "have little to tell ; but that it had a long Roman and British life no man can doubt," as Mr. Freeman told us at Carlisle in his address to the Royal Archæological Institute in 1882. It, no doubt, shared the independence of those parts of Britain from which the Roman had gone, and into which the Angle or the Saxon had not yet come. After that episode in its history, it was for two hundred years part of an English kingdom, that of the Angles of Northumberland. Again it was devastated and laid waste by Halfdene and his Danes in A.D. 875, and was, for some two hundred years before the arrival in it of William Rufus, British or nothing. " The unbroken English life of Carlisle," says Mr. Freeman, " begins with the coming of the Red King and the settlement of his English colony."

William the Red, in 1092, found Luguvallium, once a city and a fortress, a waste chester, and he refounded it as a city and a fortress. With its destruction by the Danes, the ecclesiastical establishments, whether existing at the time of the visit of St. Cuthbert in A.D. 685 or founded by him, must all have perished. Sooner or later some sort of ecclesiastical foundation was re-established in the rebuilt city, but not until long after the time of William Rufus : the ecclesiastical side of Carlisle is not the work of William Rufus, but of Henry I. The present Archdeacon of Carlisle (Dr. Prescott), in his valuable edition of the register of the Priory of Wetherhal, has proved that Henry I., on the advice of Thurstan, archbishop of York, founded in Carlisle in or about the year 1123 (and not 1102, as so frequently stated) a house of regular or Augustinian canons. This perhaps requires a little explanation, for many people believe that all ecclesiastics connected with cathedrals before the Reformation were monks. Far from it : some cathedrals were served by monks, others by canons—*i.e.*, priests who had not taken monastic vows, and who were of two kinds, secular and regular. Secular canons moved about in the world, lived in separate houses, and were similar to the canons of modern days. Regular canons, like monks, lived under the rule of some order. They were more strict than the secular canons, and lived together in common under one roof. The regular canons of St. Augustine, bishop of Hippo, from their dress, were called Black Canons; they also wore full beards. Carlisle is remarkable as being the only cathedral church that they occupied. An Englishman, as his name shows, Adulf, Athelwulf, Athelwold, prior of the Augustinian house of St. Oswald, at Nostell in Yorkshire, and confessor and chaplain to the King, was appointed first prior of Carlisle, and on the formation of the See of Carlisle in 1133 he became the first bishop. But the unbroken succession of bishops of Carlisle did not begin with the Englishman, Athelwold. After his death, in 1156, the see was vacant until 1204, when a poverty-stricken foreigner, as Dr. Prescott calls him,

was foisted upon the district by Pope Inno-
cent III., who begged the post from King
John.

Enough has now been said of the history of
the two hills of Carlisle, the Castle Hill and the
Cathedral Hill. On the first, marked out by
nature for the site of a fortress, the Red King
built, or commenced to build, while his successors finished, the fortress whose mutilated
remains, long ago divested of any strategic
importance, yet serve to shelter some small
portion of the national army. The military
first satisfied, the turn of the ecclesiastics
came; they carefully avoided the ravine
between the two hills and selected a site on
the top and along the west side of the Cathedral Hill. Tradition says that one Walter, a
wealthy Norman ecclesiastic (some say he
had formerly been a soldier), was set over the
rebuilt city by William Rufus, that he began
to build a house there, dedicated to the Virgin
Mary—a house probably of secular canons—
but, dying before he could complete the

buildings, the King in 1123 superseded the secular canons by regulars of the Order of St. Augustine, and Athelwold, the first prior, completed the structure.

The question arises, Can any part of this Walter's work be distinguished from that of Athelwold? It has been pointed out by the writer's brother, Mr. C. J. Ferguson, F. S. A., that, whereas the walls and pillars of the nave arcade of Carlisle Cathedral are of the normal thickness of Norman work, the walls of the aisles are, in strange contrast, of remarkable thinness, only about two feet four inches or thereabouts—an indication of pre-Norman work. It seems to point to a building, so far as the outer walls, on older foundations. Now we can hardly imagine those older foundations to have belonged to some church destroyed by the Danes in 875 : Carlisle could at that time hardly have possessed a church with a nave as wide as the nave that we now see. We are driven then to the time of the Red King : he brought from the south

Among the Ruins

artificers, including, no doubt, builders skilled in the Norman fashion of building. But these masons would be employed upon the King's work, upon the fortifications, while Walter would have to employ such local talent as he could get—Britons, Celts and Irish—who would adhere to their old fashion of building thin walls, compared with those the Normans were in the habit of building. Thirty years later, when Athelwold took up Walter's work, he would insist upon the grand Norman pillars and walls of the nave arcade that now win our admiration, though he might not care for the expense of putting in new and wider foundations for the aisle walls. The thinness of these walls implies a stone construction or mason work, whereas the walls of the keep of Carlisle Castle are of concrete and of great thickness. Thus it is clear that the thin aisle walls of the nave of Carlisle Cathedral and the thick walls of the keep of Carlisle Castle are the work of building artificers trained in different schools;

the Norman artificers who built the keep having derived their method of building in concrete from the Romans, while the masons who built the aisle walls came from a race unaffected by the Roman traditions of building, and possibly Irish. A curious corroboration of this suggestion was obtained in 1892, when the foundations of an ancient feretory or apse, projected from the eastern face of the north transept of Athelwold's Norman church which preceded the present choir, were exposed in some work connected with the organ. The circular wall of the apse, at a level of about three feet below the present floor-level, is about four feet three inches thick, and made entirely of stone, dressed with a hatchet, built stone to stone, with no sign of concrete, and so differing from the usual Norman fashion. Here we have proof that Athelwold, prior and bishop, had to follow in the footsteps of Walter, and to employ the local talent, and not the Norman builders imported by William II.

The Nave

Putting aside these speculations, let us, before going into detail, take a very rapid survey of the existing church or churches, for there were two churches within the one building ; let us then see if we can pick out what remains of the church or churches built by Athelwold the Englishman, prior and bishop of Carlisle.

The Cathedral, structurally, now consists of a fragmentary nave and aisles, two bays only remaining ; aisleless transepts with a chapel on the east side of the southern one ; a choir with aisle and processional path, and a central tower.

The original church—i.e., Athelwold's church—was a Norman minster of the twelfth century, of moderate size, of which there are still fragments to be seen. These consist of the two eastern bays of the nave (those to the west having been destroyed in 1646) ; of the south transept, almost entire ; and of the lower half of the piers that support the central tower. The nave formerly extended much further to the west ; it had several more bays or compartments, and the foundations of its west wall were discovered a few years ago buried behind the house belonging to the second prebendal stall, somewhere under the floor of the present greenhouse. Athelwold's choir was very small compared with the magnificent one that now exists : the foundations of its east end were uncovered during the restoration in the time of Dean Tait. It proved to be apsidal or circular at the end, and eighty feet in length ; as the length of the nave is one-hundred-and-forty-one feet, and the tower is thirty-five feet square, we get the total internal length of Athelwold's, or the Norman cathedral, as two-hundred-and-fifty-six feet.

Doubts have been entertained, and by high authorities, as to whether the western bays of the Norman church ever existed ; but such doubts are without any basis. It is needless in this little booklet to discuss the evidence for their former existence ; suffice it to say that Dr. Todd, prebendary of Carlisle, writing in 1688, positively states of the Parliamentary officers: "The westward of St. Mary's Church they demolished, which was afterwards built shorter as it now stands." Dr. Todd had ample means of knowing, for in 1688 there must have been in Carlisle plenty of persons, both ecclesiastics and laymen, who could recollect the western bays in existence prior to 1646. The bishop, Dr. Smith, to whom Todd had long been chaplain, was an Appleby man by birth, born in 1615, fond of architecture, and must have known the nave of Athelwold's church prior to its mutilation. Further there is in the library at Lambeth a survey of the year 1649, which says: "It appears onto us by ye view of judicious workmen that ye decayes of the church of S. Maryes of Carlyle is such that ye weste pte being taken down the repair of the east will coste fyve hundred pounds att ye Least wch seems to us very necessarye their beeinge but one other church (wch is likewise very Ruynous) in all that Citty," &c.

This Norman minster was one of the instances of divided possession—that is, of two churches in one building. At Carlisle it probably arose in this way: Walter the Norman and the secular canons who came with him, or followed him, and afterwards the Austin canons, undertook the ecclesiastical organisation of the rebuilt city and of the district. These last, as was usual with Austin canons, established a congregation in the nave of their church, retaining the choir for their own services. In course of time the congregation in the nave acquired rights therein, and the nave became their parish church —St. Mary's Parish Church. Some have, however, indulged in a theory that there was in Carlisle a separate church dedicated to St. Mary, which the Scots burnt, whereon the parishioners were allowed to take refuge in the nave of the Cathedral. This is pure romance; the Scots never burnt any church in Carlisle.

A misapprehension prevails as to the division between the church of the canons and the parish church. Prior to 1871 the parish church occupied the existing bays of the nave, which were cut off from the rest of the building by a wall under the west arch of the tower. Many persons have too hastily concluded that the parish church had always been in this position, but that prior to 1646 it had included the whole length of the unmutilated nave. A little reflection will show that this is an untenable idea. All the evidence we possess shows that the eastern arm of the Norman minster was very short indeed—only 80 feet; it follows that the ritualist choir of the canons must have extended under the tower arches into the nave, as at Gloucester, Norwich, Winchester, and St. Alban's; this is proved at Carlisle by the fact that the faces of the piers of the central tower, towards the central axis of the building, are built flat for the reception of the woodwork of the canons' stalls. The lower part, moreover, of the wall that at present terminates the nave is over five feet thick, pointing to its being a very old wall—mediæval, indeed, as far as the lower portion is concerned; the upper part is a modern make-up. At Gloucester the pulpitum or rood screen occupied exactly the same position as the present west wall of Carlisle, thus enclosing the two eastern bays of the nave. There is some evidence that the present west wall of Carlisle Cathedral once had in it the central door which distinguishes a rood screen from a reredos. Thus we may well come to the conclusion that the choir of the canons extended nearly to the present west end of the church, and that the original church of St. Mary's parish was to the westward of that end, and was entirely demolished in 1646. The necessary funds for its rebuilding not being forthcoming, the parish church was then huddled ("huddled" is the word, as those who recollect it prior to 1871 will recognise) into the two remaining bays of the nave.

North Transept
and Tower, Restored

A⋆A

Athelwold's minster must have witnessed some stately functions within its walls; Carlisle was not then, as now, unused to royal visits. On the death of Henry I., that city was handed over to the old king of Scots, David I., as the price of his acquiescence in the usurpation by Stephen of the English crown. At Carlisle David held his court, and at Carlisle he received more than one papal legate. To him, at Carlisle, resorted Prince Henry, the future Henry II. of England, then a lad of sixteen. At Carlisle Prince Henry remained for eight months, and while there the ceremony of knighting him was performed with great pomp in the presence of many grandees, both English and Scotch. At Carlisle, too, there was held in King David's time a synod of Scottish bishops, at which Athelwold of Carlisle was present. At Carlisle, in 1158, Henry II. and Malcolm, king of the Scots, met, but parted, unable to adjust their differences. At Carlisle, again, in 1186,

Henry II. met William the Lion, king of the Scots, and entertained him in a most friendly manner.

All these occasions must have afforded opportunities for stately and sumptuous ecclesiastical pageants, in which the authorities of the Norman minster would do the best that their small and somewhat cramped choir admitted ; but for what they did we must draw upon our imagination, as documentary evidence does not, to our knowledge, remain. Other ceremonies were done in that Norman minster which could hardly be called pageants, for in them the poor trembling canons had to take part under fear of present death if they refused, and the certainty of future punishment if they acquiesced. Thus, in 1216, Carlisle was surrendered to William the Lion, who was then under papal excommunication ; yet he compelled the canons of Carlisle, under fear of death, to say mass for him, and also to elect *quemdam clericum suum interdictum et excommunicatum*, as their bishop and pastor. For these their sins they were presently driven into exile by Gualio, the papal legate, and the Pope's mandate was issued for the election, with the royal assent, of Hugh Abbot of Beaulieu, to be the third bishop of Carlisle.

This then is the story of the Norman minster, built by Athelwold the Englishman; for in the thirteenth century the canons rebuilt the choir on a much larger scale. We have already mentioned, rather by anticipation than in chronological order, how the west part of the nave was pulled down in 1646. Let us now pause awhile in our story, and linger over the architectural details of the fragment that remains of the Norman minster.

On the outside of the nave, the dark grey rectangular blocks of stone, of which it is largely built, from their tooling and general appearance, are supposed, and rightly so, to have come from that ready quarry, the

Roman wall; of its wealth of dressed stone, the mediæval masons who built Carlisle Castle and Cathedral freely availed themselves, putting their own masons' marks upon the Roman tooling. The transept and the north aisle of the nave have the usual flat Norman pilaster buttresses, dying into the cornice, which in the aisle is carried upon a series of plain corbels. The clerestories of the nave have no buttresses, but the cornice runs in an unbroken line here and in the transept, supported by grotesque heads. The windows display the characteristic Norman ornaments—the zigzag, chevron, billet, &c. The lower part of the south transept is much plainer than any other portion of the building, and the buttresses are omitted along the south aisle wall, as that wall would be covered by the conventual buildings.

Entering by the great modern door, where no door was of old, the spectator's eye is at once attracted by the distorted condition of

Distorted Arches
in the Nave

the arches which carry the central tower. This distortion is due to the piers of the tower, unequal to the superimposed weight, having shortly after their erection telescoped into the earth about a foot. Near the door in the south transept a glass covers a Runic scribble, which means, "Dolfin wrote these runes"—a scribble by some workman, which formerly would be concealed by paint, plaster, or tapestry.

No fabric rolls exist for Carlisle Cathedral from which we can derive information : we must gather what we can from the building itself. But as the Church in England grew wealthier, so its ritual grew more sumptuous and demanded for its display a larger area than afforded by the somewhat small and cramped Norman choirs ; these were generally rebuilt, in the then prevalent style of architecture, to suit the new requirements. At Carlisle this seems to have been commenced, judging from the details of the choir, in the bishopric of Silvester de

Everdon, 1245 to 1255. The work was con-
tinued by Everdon's successors, Bishops
Vipont, De Chauncy, and De Irton. The
last named, who died on March 1, 1292,
converted his visitations into the means of
extorting large sums of money from his
clergy for the purposes of the work at the
Cathedral; the writer of the "Chronicle of
Lanercost" waxes very indignant about this,
and calls the bishop "*admodum cupidus*,"
"*prædo, non præsul*," "*improbus exactor*,"
and such-like bad names. John de Halucton,
or de Haloghton (best known as Bishop
Halton) was elected to the vacant see on
St. George's Day (April 23) following. On
the 30th of the next month a dire misfortune
befell his Cathedral and Cathedral city. A
tremendous gale, evidently from the west,
blew for twenty-four hours, parching up the
vegetation, forcing men and horses off the
roads, and driving the sea over Burgh and
Rockcliff marshes, higher than had ever
been known before, to the destruction of

large numbers of cattle and sheep. In the midst of this terrible storm an incendiary set fire to his father's house, which was just outside the city, near the west end of the Cathedral ; the flames spread, and the whole city and suburbs were destroyed, with the exception of a few houses and the church of the Black Friars. Graphic accounts, both in prose and verse, of this catastrophe are contained in the "Chronicle of Lanercost." From the special mention made of the destruction of the bells and organs in the Cathedral, we judge they must have been such as the canons might well be proud of.

Mr. Purday, clerk of the works during the restoration in Dean Tait's time, in an able but now rare tract on Carlisle Cathedral, gives it as his opinion that the remains of the new choir left by the fire are the outside walls of the north and south aisles (with the exception of the eastern bay on each side), the whole of St. Catherine's Chapel, and the arch at the west end of the north aisle opening into the transept. In fact, the grand new choir was completely wrecked, except the side aisle walls, which Mr. Purday conjectures were protected by their stone vaultings.

Of Athelwold's work the nave escaped, but the fire destroyed the north transept, injured the south transept walls, and almost annihilated the conventual buildings. The central tower was also much damaged.

A question has been raised whether at the date of this fire the rebuilding of the choir, started by De Everdon, had so far progressed as that the roof was on. Mr. Purday thinks that it must have been, "as the almost total ruin which succeeded that event could scarcely have been brought about unless the building had contained a large quantity of combustible materials such as a roof of this extent would supply." The Bishop of London (Dr. Creighton), in "Carlisle," Historic Towns series, suggests that the work had only been carried up to the tops of the main arches and that a temporary wooden roof had been

The Transept
and Intersection

thrown over the unfinished building at that
level. Dr. Creighton evidently thinks that
had the permanent roof been in place it would
have been of stone; but Mr. Freeman told the
Archæological Institute at Carlisle, in 1882,
that the choir was from the very first designed
for a wooden roof.

De Everdon's choir, longer and broader
than the Norman choir, was not symmetrically
placed with regard to the Norman nave, its
central line being removed to the northwards
of that of the nave—a displacement rendered
necessary by the existence on the south side
of the conventual buildings. Internally this
was a matter of no moment, as the screens,
dividing the building into two churches, concealed it ; externally the eccentricity of nave
and choir is cleverly disguised by a subsidiary
turret alongside of the great tower for part of
its height, and by a pepper-box turret on its
summit. Whether it was intended to rebuild
the whole Cathedral in accordance with the
new choir is uncertain. Preparations were

made for rebuilding the north transept, as shown by the pillar at the west end of the north aisle and the fragment of wall on the outside in that vicinity. But it may well be that those who rebuilt on so magnificent a scale the canons' church in the architectural choir of the building cared nothing about the parochial church in the nave, and that the parish had scant funds to devote to such purposes.

Low indeed must the hearts of the canons of Carlisle have sunk within them : their beautiful choir, which had taken half a century to rear, had become a black and ghastly wreck, and that too just as they were nearing its completion: they were burnt out, roofless and homeless. It was all the harder upon them because they had aimed at having the very best of work, boldness of style, and the utmost beauty of detail. It was all thrown away. Could they have looked into the future and seen the dismal vista before them of about a century and a half of Scottish wars, of their bishops turned to soldiers, and

The Eastern End.

of plundered and ruined churches, they must have despaired. But the future, its misery and poverty, they could not foresee ; but ever, though misery and poverty befell them, they struggled bravely on, determined to still insist on the very best of work, on boldness of style, and on the utmost beauty of design, even if they had to wait a hundred years.

The rebuilding was, however, long in doing : times were troublous, and Scottish wars little favourable for the collection of subscriptions. The conventual buildings would be first rebuilt as rapidly as possible, for the sake of shelter, and nothing more spent upon them than was absolutely necessary. The transept followed, but the rebuilding of the choir extended over many years, and a long stop was made after the cill of the triforium was reached. The building must have been in a very sad condition when, in 1297, Robert Bruce swore fealty to Edward I. on the sword of St. Thomas before Bishop Halton in Carlisle Cathedral. Nor can it have been far advanced in the rebuilding in January 1306-7, when the Prince of Wales, the Archbishop of York, nineteen bishops, thrice that number of mitred abbots, a large number of the most powerful barons of the realm, and the great officers of State attended the Parliament of Carlisle. To Carlisle also came Cardinal Petrus Hispanus (Peter l'Espagnol), the papal legate. He preached in the Cathedral at Carlisle, and " revested himselfe and the other bishops which were present, and then, with candels light and causing the bels to be roong, they accursed, in terrible wise, Robert Bruce, the vsurper of the crowne of Scotland, with all his partakers, aiders and mainteiners."—Holinshed, ii. 523. About midsummer another stately ceremony took place in Carlisle Cathedral. Edward I. made there a solemn offering of the horse litter in which he had travelled to the north and of the horses belonging to it.

Building was resumed under Bishops Welton (1352-62) and Appleby (1362-95), who made strenuous efforts to raise funds ; to these Edward III. and many of the nobility contributed, and the work was brought to a successful conclusion before the death of Edward III. in 1377. To these two bishops may be attributed the whole of the east end above the aisle roofs, and also the triforium, clerestory and roof of the choir, which was wagon-shaped of panelled wood, with great hammer beams, from which it is probable large lamps were suspended. It was curiously painted, and adorned with bosses, on which were blazoned the arms of the noble families who had subscribed to the rebuilding. A list of them is preserved in the College of Arms.

Dr. Creighton considers the absence of a stone vaulted roof a sign of enforced economy, but Mr. Freeman considers that the roof was always intended to be of wood, and points out that "the English tradition of making a wooden roof an ornamental feature was here to be seen on the greatest scale." In support of Mr. Freeman, it may be pointed out that no provision was made for taking the thrust of a vaulted roof, either by flying buttresses or otherwise. Mr. Freeman also said the east window of Carlisle " was the grandest of its kind in England, and he supposed in the world. There was as big a window in one of the churches in Perugia which in some points reminded him of this; but here they had the finest piece of tracery to be seen anywhere."

The active misfortunes of the Cathedral did not end with the fire of 1292 : it suffered from a second fire in 1392, which destroyed the front of the north transept. Little written record remains of this fire, but the front tells its own story—the story of damage by fire, repaired with the utmost economy, the old materials being re-used, and broken stones being patched, instead of being re-placed. This was probably the work of Bishop Strickland (bishop, 1400-19); he also built the tower upon the distorted Norman piers. Foundations so ticklish necessi-

tated caution as to the weights to be put upon them, and hence the tower, built in short stages, is somewhat stunted. It had originally a short spire of wood, covered with lead, but this was taken down in the last century.

Bishop Strickland placed in the tower four bells, of which one now remains there. The stalls in the choir are also the work of this bishop, but the tabernacle work over them is attributed to Prior Haithwaite, *circa* 1433 or later. The armorial bearings and the images which once adorned them have all disappeared. To Bishop Strickland the completion of the fabric, if ever it may be considered to have been complete, may be attributed.

The internal decoration of the building was largely due to two priors: Thomas Gondibour, who was appointed in 1484, and Lancelot Salkeld, the last prior and first dean. To the first are due the curious paintings at the back of the stalls, representing the legends of St. Augustine, St. Anthony, and

St. Cuthbert, and the figures of the twelve Apostles. For long these were covered with whitewash. Both Gondibour and Salkeld put into the church some beautiful wooden screens; the remains of Gondibour's screens enclose St. Catherine's Chapel. Salkeld's screens, of beautiful Renaissance work, are between the chancel and the north aisle. The building was probably at its best just before the Reformation; the interior was gorgeously gilt and painted, the walls, capitals, and tabernacle work enriched with colour, and the windows glorious with stained glass, of which little now remains. Much was probably taken out at the Reformation, when also the images from the tabernacle work would disappear and the paintings at the back of the stalls be whitewashed. Little wanton mischief would be done : the change at Carlisle was a peaceable one. The prior and canons of the Augustinian house became the dean and canons of a cathedral of the new foundation, but they were poor. Suc-

Prior Slee's Gateway

ceeding deans, two at least, were non-resident laymen, and the place was neglected and let run down. From the oft-quoted journal of three officers from Norwich, who were upon a tour through northern England, we get a melancholy picture of the Cathedral in 1634 : "The next day we repaired to their cathedral, which is nothing near so fair and stately as those we had seen, but more like a great wild country church ; and as it appeared outwardly so was it inwardly, ne'er beautiful nor adorned one whit. The organ and voices did well agree, the one being like a shrill bagpipe, the other like a Scottish tune. The sermon in the like accent was such as we could hardly bring away, though it was delivered by a neat young scholar, sent that morning from Rose Castle, the bishop's mansion, which lies upon Rose and Caldew rivers—one of the bishop's chaplains—to supply his place that day. The Communion was also administered and received in a wild unreverent manner."

# Carlisle Cathedral

The destruction at Carlisle was wrought after the surrender of the city to General Lesley in 1646, when the chapter-house, and other conventual buildings, and several bays of the nave were pulled down. During the Commonwealth the building was the scene of much rioting : the " terrible man with the leather breeches," George Fox, preached there, and the church had to be cleared of a riotous mob by files of musketeers. In 1746 the Cathedral was degraded into a prison for the captured Highlanders and was left in a filthy condition. Then followed a destructive restoration under Bishop Lyttleton. During this a plaster ceiling was inserted below the oak one, exquisite wooden screens were torn out, and the space between the stalls was filled up with pews.

In 1853 extensive restoration was commenced under Mr. Christian ; and later still, in 1871, under Mr. Street, the pews were pulled out, and the fragment of the nave thrown open to the rest of the church.

# Carlisle Cathedral

The only old glass in the church is that in the upper part of the glorious east window. This represents a doom—that is, our Lord sitting in judgment; the procession of the blessed to the palace of heaven; the place of punishment of the wicked and the general resurrection. In one of the quatrefoils of the tracery, just above the mullions, is a figure surrounded by an heraldic border, golden castles and leopards' faces alternately—a border of Castile and Leon. This points to John of Gaunt, who was Governor of Carlisle from 1380 to 1384, and who impaled Castile and Leon in right of his wife; this is probably his portrait. It also gives the date of the glass as between 1380 and 1384.

Of modern glass in the building, by far the best is that over the door in the south transept, representing the Seven Days of the Creation; each symbolised by an angel holding a roundel, on which are depicted the events of the day.

# Carlisle Cathedral

We have almost forgotten to call attention to what never fails to interest. The capitals of the columns in the choir have been "wrought with a grace," says Dr. Creighton, "that makes them exquisite examples of ornamentation. Twelve of them take for their motive the representation of the months of the year : a motive common enough, but nowhere wrought out with so much luxuriance of fancy. The groundwork of the figures is foliage clustering round the tops of the pillars ; oaks extend their branches and vines send forth their shoots. These are peopled by birds and beasts, by men and grotesque creatures in every attitude, but always full of life and movement. On the spaces facing the choir are placed the representations of the months, showing the various occupations of the different seasons—now a peasant pulling off his wet boots and warming his bare feet at the fire ; now a lord riding out with his hand full of roses and a hawk upon his fist ; now a reaper and again a sower—the whole

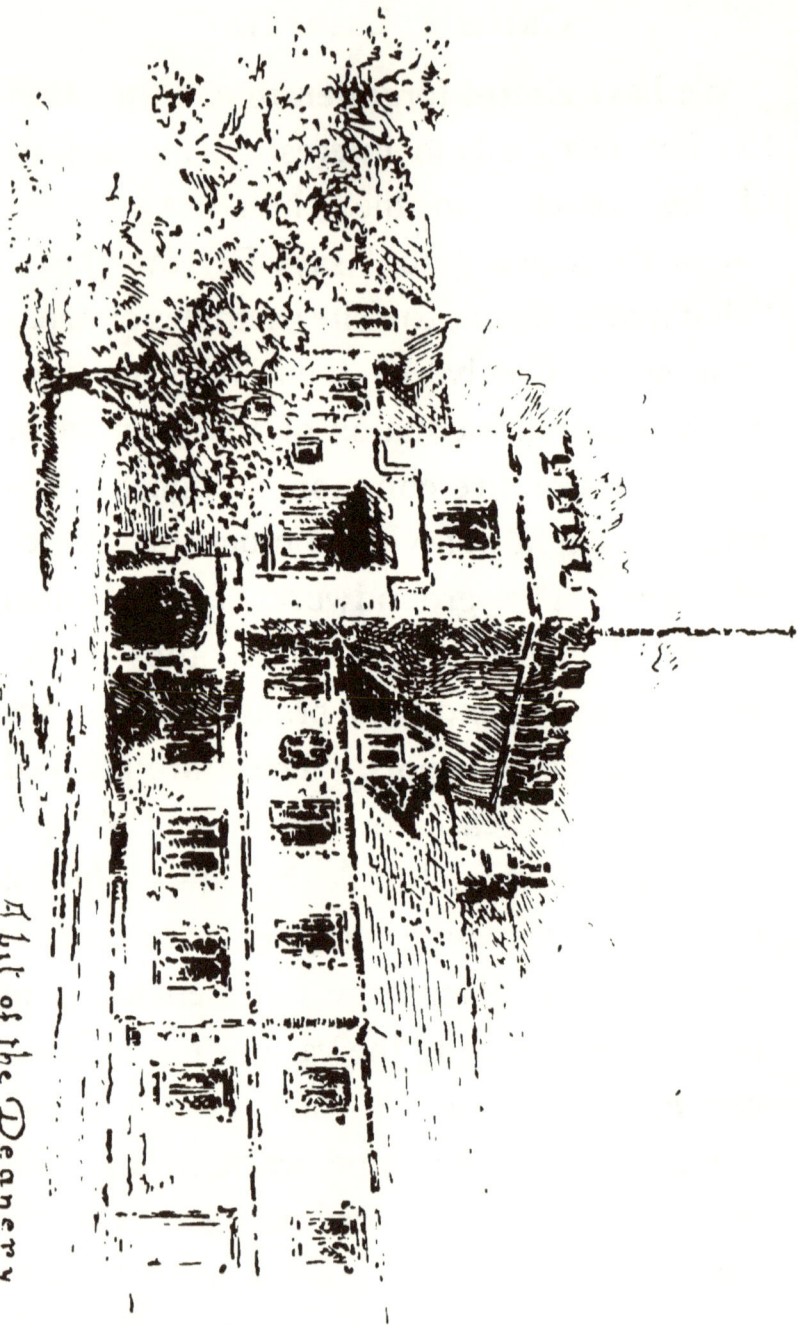

A bit of the Deanery

presenting a picture of rural England of the time." The series begins with the second column from the east on the south side; a figure with three faces under one hood, two of which are busy drinking, represents January.

Twenty bishops of Carlisle lie buried in their Cathedral, from De Everdon, who died *circa* 1255, to Law, who died in 1787. To only seven of these do any monuments remain, namely, two effigies doubtfully assigned to Irton (d. 1292) and to Barrow (d. 1429): the last is by St. Catherine's Chapel, opposite to Thornycroft's fine effigy of Bishop Goodwin, and is evidently a portrait. Bishop Bell (d. 1496) has a fine brass in the centre of the choir, and Bishop Robinson (d. 1616) a curious one, now in the north aisle. The other monuments are on the walls or in the floor. Archdeacon Paley lies in the north aisle, and forgotten deans, chancellors and prebendaries are frequent. Two of the Lords Dacre of the North were buried in Carlisle

Cathedral—Lord William on December 14, 1563, and Lord Thomas on July 25, 1566; but neither monument nor tradition records their graves.

Of the conventual buildings but little remains. The great gatehouse to the west was the work of Prior Christopher Slee in 1528. The Prior's lodging is now the deanery and contains a curiously painted ceiling, the work of Prior Simon Senos (Senhouse). The fratry or refectory completes the list of conventual buildings that remain : the cloisters, dormitories, chapter-house and other accessories of a house of canons are all gone, barely leaving sufficient fragments to indicate their positions.

*Printed by* BALLANTYNE, HANSON & CO
*London & Edinburgh*

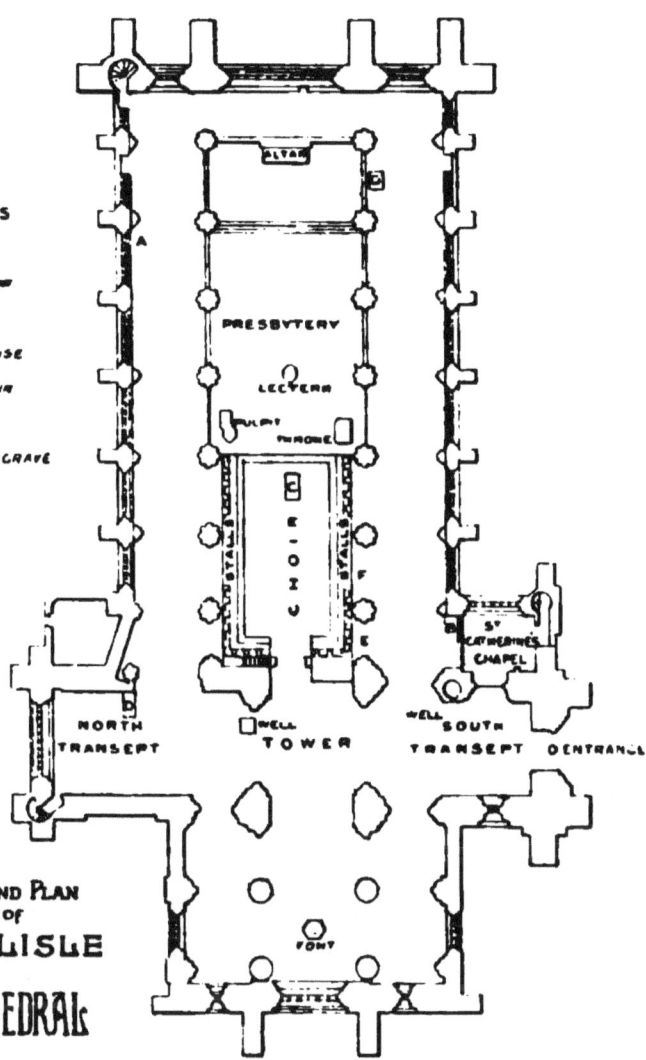

MONUMENTS

A  Bishop Irton
B  Bishop Barrow
C  Bishop Bell
D  Prior Senhouse
E  Bishop Goodwin
F  Dean Close
G  Bishop Waldegrave

ALTAR

PRESBYTERY

LECTERN

PULPIT

THRONE

STALLS

CHOIR

STALLS

ST CATHERINE'S CHAPEL

NORTH TRANSEPT

WELL

TOWER

WELL

SOUTH TRANSEPT

ENTRANCE

FONT

GROUND PLAN
of
CARLISLE
CATHEDRAL